IT'S TIME TO LEARN ABOUT APATOSAURUSES

It's Time to Learn about Apatosauruses

Walter the Educator

Silent King Books
A WhichHead Entertainment Imprint

Copyright © 2025 by Walter the Educator

All rights reserved. No part of this book may be reproduced in any manner whatsoever without written per- mission except in the case of brief quotations embodied in critical articles and reviews.

First Printing, 2024

Disclaimer

This book is a literary work; the story is not about specific persons, locations, situations, and/or circumstances unless mentioned in a historical context. Any resemblance to real persons, locations, situations, and/or circumstances is coincidental. This book is for entertainment and informational purposes only. The author and publisher offer this information without warranties expressed or implied. No matter the grounds, neither the author nor the publisher will be accountable for any losses, injuries, or other damages caused by the reader's use of this book. The use of this book acknowledges an understanding and acceptance of this disclaimer.

It's Time to Learn about Apatosauruses is a collectible early learning book by Walter the Educator suitable for all ages belonging to Walter the Educator's Time to Eat Book Series. Collect more books at WaltertheEducator.com

USE THE EXTRA SPACE TO TAKE NOTES AND DOCUMENT YOUR MEMORIES

APATOSAURUSES

Long ago, in days of old,

It's Time to Learn about
Apatosauruses

When dinosaurs were brave and bold,

Lived Apatosaurus, big and tall,

One of the largest of them all!

With legs so thick and strong and stout,

It stomped the land as it walked about.

Its neck stretched high, so long and lean,

To reach the leaves so fresh and green.

A tiny head on a neck so wide,

With little teeth tucked inside.

It didn't bite, it didn't chew,

It swallowed plants, quite a few!

Its tail was long, so strong and thin,

Like a whip to help defend.

If danger came, it'd swing it fast,

A mighty snap to make threats pass!

It's Time to Learn about
Apatosauruses

It lived in herds, not all alone,

Together they would graze and roam.

From rivers wide to forests tall,

They searched for plants to eat them all!

No meat for them, just plants and trees,

A gentle giant, if you please!

It munched on ferns and leaves so high,

Reaching branches in the sky.

Eggs so big, like giant stones,

Kept safe among the trees and bones.

A baby hatched, so small and new,

But quickly grew, as dinos do!

With feet like pillars, firm and round,

It shook the earth and shook the ground.

Though slow it walked, it had no fear,

It's Time to Learn about
Apatosauruses

Its mighty size made threats stay clear!

Though it lived so long ago,

Its fossils help us learn and know.

Bones so big, so strong, so tall,

Tell the tale of times for all.

So if you hear of days gone past,

When dinosaurs were strong and vast,

Remember this grand, gentle friend,

It's Time to Learn about Apatosauruses

Apatosaurus, from start to end!

ABOUT THE CREATOR

Walter the Educator is one of the pseudonyms for Walter Anderson. Formally educated in Chemistry, Business, and Education, he is an educator, an author, a diverse entrepreneur, and he is the son of a disabled war veteran. "Walter the Educator" shares his time between educating and creating. He holds interests and owns several creative projects that entertain, enlighten, enhance, and educate, hoping to inspire and motivate you. Follow, find new works, and stay up to date with Walter the Educator™ at WaltertheEducator.com

www.ingramcontent.com/pod-product-compliance
Lightning Source LLC
LaVergne TN
LVHW052017060526
838201LV00059B/4064